HAPPINESS THREADS

THE UNBORN POEMS

HAPPINESS THREADS
THE UNBORN POEMS

Melanie Dennis Unrau

The
Muses'
Company

Happiness Threads: The Unborn Poems
first published 2013 by
The Muses' Company
An imprint of J. Gordon Shillingford Publishing Inc.

The Muses' Company Series Editor: Clarise Foster
Cover design by Terry Gallagher/Doowah Design Inc.
Interior design by Relish New Brand Experience
Author photo by Jason Unrau
Cover art by Brenna George
Printed and bound in Canada on 100% post-consumer recycled paper.

We acknowledge the financial support of the Manitoba Arts Council and The Canada Council for the Arts for our publishing program.

Library and Archives Canada Cataloguing in Publication

Unrau, Melanie Dennis, 1979-, author
Happiness threads : the unborn poems / Melanie Dennis Unrau.

ISBN 978-1-897289-95-2 (pbk.)

I. Title.

PS8641.N744H36 2013 C811'.6 C2013-903311-4

J. Gordon Shillingford Publishing
P.O. Box 86, RPO Corydon Avenue, Winnipeg, MB Canada R3M 3S3

To all of my mothers—Jeanette, Elaine, Nim, Mo, Grace, and Jane—for loving me, and for showing me how.

TABLE OF CONTENTS

my children are not my poetry
                                        so beautiful
they make their own

i let the houseplants die
because i can
wear the same clothes all week
cheesecake
chocolate
nachos
sleep

i lost my poems
this one is not a child

wrap myself in blankets that still
smell of breastmilk   wish for it back then
cry for my losses
who am i now

it's always work to be awake   push
back against routine   stoop to play
a child's game   while the laundry the dishes i
go unwashed and unwritten

a mother's job is to know
what matters and keep it alive

a poet's job is to feel
for a pulse

so long as i'm living
                    it is

ONE
little bird

enceinte

you were so careful never
to fall lift never think
dark thoughts

the sea parted for you every morning
down portage avenue on the walk to work
you cradled your belly
contemplated its sweet yolk

people will say it just wasn't meant to be
but they don't know how you dreamt
hot bath nicotine
a sip of wine
slip on the ice
tumble down the stairs

maybe you couldn't help it
but when you're splayed here
at the bottom of consciousness
what you wanted and didn't want
saw coming and didn't
what you felt and when you stopped feeling

well, you just can't tell anymore

miscarriage

you remember the time
the boys down the street used hockey sticks
to knock a robin's nest to the ground
& you cupped that little bird in your hands

d & c

every step sounds unbearable
watch the midwife's face as she searches
for a heartbeat   see the body
float on the dark screen

drugged into labour   spread your legs
for indifferent interns   pace
the halls of blame the long hours of loneliness
wait for your body to release its grip

try your best to breathe
like you've seen in the movies
& when it's over hold him
this will be the only time

by now you know what you can bear
lay yourself on the operating table   veins
sucking on the dry needle   music
humming on the stereo & whisper

empty me

still

these days all i write is:

brown

umbilical   rot

  blood

ears

                              those little fingers

crushed

fish   eyes

    unborn

unborn poems

i went out looking for them
but forgot what i was looking for
& lost them twice

– Debbie Keahey

i.

the unborn are into telepathy   e.s.p.   &
out-of-body experience
you sense them hovering over you
when your breasts ache & you hold
your empty belly

the voices in your head are tiny
brown hands caressing your
sorrow wearing it down to something more
bearable   they
never meant to hurt you
they had no idea

this is how they leave   slip
out of their bodies
to feel what it is to be free
of your droning heartbeat

sometimes they never come back

ii.

the unborn never die
like in that old gospel song
they fly away

in the limbo of womb   they dreamt
of an end   anything
they took the easy way out

now you hope they dream of you
wake with arms & legs flailing   reaching
to touch your insides
& you are not there

iii.

the midwife told you sometimes
the unborn dissolve
absorbed back into their mothers   they
like it that way
to leave without a trace
become the only person
they ever loved

iv.

his body was brown & empty
skin clung to our fingers
when we tried to pull away
the nurse took him from us   i cried
as if this parting & not some
silent trauma
were the moment of his death

you can't take the unborn home
your breasts may leak
but he is not hungry

he is a polaroid   guesses about eyes
a useless name a strange smell
that lingers   the sound of the
doppler machine   searching

he is the silence
between my heartbeats

birth control

this morning you lay in bed
convinced you were pregnant
you could feel it
hungry   tired
you were not alone

you got up to find the red spots
of clockwork on your pants
your rhythm timed to the dial of pills
prescribed by the obstetrician who said
it's a good idea to wait a few months

you will wait more than a few months
you are pulling your life together
you will work   go back to school
you need time

wound like a watch
you tick away twenty-one days a month
in efficiency & sound judgment
but for one free week you live in hope

that there has been a mistake
you have become a one percent rate of error
& this one will live

anniversaire

the other children were born
on their birthdays grew
into their clothing
slept in their nurseries
we watch as they distance themselves
from the hospital pictures
the closed eyes

but the child in this picture is as still
as he was a year ago his body
a shadow on the too-big blanket
he will fade in our memory
become the sediment over which we float
our new hopes

TWO
little pumpkin

expecting

dusty streets beg for a pin prick
to the bloated belly of sky

plants clench to break
through soil hard as concrete
reach the surface, exhale
tender green arms

spring swims within us
waiting to break out
in daffodils, rain,
our secret news

the womb is

heaven where god
sits carefully
knitting socks

hung with cords like clotheslines
my first child
died tangled in its hair

an ocean the child paddles
curve of belly a horizon
my voice her compass

never quiet
my heart thuds the child
yawns testing her voice

a nightmare nine months
of falling no idea what it is
to land

warm the child could stay
forever breathing liquid
dreaming air

december 31

i wake
slick and swollen
20 minutes before the alarm

the arithmetic of the calendar will crumble
at midnight when we count down
a year in 10 seconds

the bassinet beside our bed is still empty
and i am tired of counting
contractions   the syllables of names

tomorrow pulls like gravity
and the child settles
in my hips

for her the year will turn
at birth   40 weeks
one day old

second coat

at midnight i make it back to the window
realize those branches brush
the side of the house like the snores
of a congested child
and i've been listening all night

concrete

i am the sidewalk where
she makes me write her name
over and over

she never asks for mine
i write it in myself
dare the rain to try and erase it

favour

the price we paid was crooked
teeth hand-me-downs no walkmen
and no disneyworld
in the schoolyard we traded homemade pie
for oreos and fruit snacks

mom spared no expense
affection came easy and in a deep dish
made from scratch
ingredients gleaned from the bargain bin
or bought half off and with a coupon

dishpan hands sized my bangs for a trim
shaped rosebuds on a birthday cake
smacked a bare bum asking for it
sliced her dreams thin then
served them for dinner:
no bitter aftertaste just a mouthful of home

no woman wants to become her mother
but it's her i conjure as i stir-soup-sing-a-nursery-
rhyme-step-over-the-legos-on-the-kitchen-floor
her silent regret i cup with the ambition
that flutters like a moth between my palms
alive for now
her judgment as i tote a sick child
to the boardroom fist full of crayons
her angel i wrestle:
bless me

THREE
little guy

a birth story

baby world the welcome say you
legs two see you
arms two see you
mouth a see you
eyes two see you
eye one see you
born be baby my will when say you
tummy your in baby am i
and tree in live we
bananas eat we
monkeys are we pretend ok?
tummies or eggs from come monkeys do
mommy

reclining buddha

i.

when her son came home to the village
pickup truck full of soliders   guns
the cambodian woman who wanted me to call her mother
took my only light
neighbours whispered lock your door
so i sat all night under the mosquito net in pitch-black terror

i don't remember the men who must have laid
on the floors i crept along first thing next morning
as the temple monks chanted on the loudspeaker
i found my flip-flops in the patchwork of shoes
at the base of the stairs
were they clutching AK-47s even then?

i do remember a pause at a threshold
where he slept in the family bed
still in uniform
mother's arm slung over his chest

she'd tell me later it was all he wanted
to tuck his grown body into her the way the small
children did nights after supper when dishes were done
and women lounged on the bamboo floor
lay like he used to before
pol pot before hunger the *pey um*[1]

she slept better too with a child
to ground her
still as a statue but warm
enlightenment coursing through her like milk

it was the first time i saw them   *may* and *koen*[2]
positions of our deepest knowledge
and craving

---

1 the Cambodian military police.
2 mother and child

ii.

when you come to my bed with your
whimpers and needs
bird mouth searching for my breast
i know i will hold you the rest of the night

cup your bald head
in my hands soft
round smelling of birth and
my scent which comes stronger now
so you will know me so
your head will stink like
armpit from spending each night
here with me

reclining mother breasts
emptying at your smallest
cry warm sweet too much
for wise little you who let it stream
out the side of your mouth so
we wake each morning soaked
in my love your only food

iii.

some nights, he tries to hold his own child
the way he thinks
a woman—not his mother—
wound her soft womb around him
and slept

iv.

at three years i can hold
the whole curve of your belly
in my hand cup your calf in my palm
nightly you cry for me
i lay out my sleepy flesh your hand
finds its place on my bare shoulder

whatever we are during the day we are both
unborn in this liquid room

another birth story

I am a woman giving birth to myself.—Adrienne Rich

i am eighteen hours long
i like to feel me
open sharp and terrible
i give the word:
a death
a birth

his body passes through
viscous like cool
jelly in the throat

first a cry

then i send the placenta
fold myself in

back to school
the lackers
and the lackeys
fuckers and the fucked
woman in the seminar
who whispers
girly parts
a phallus a hole

it's hidden in plain sight
so everyone needs
one, a hand-held mirror
two, a diagram—neat lines
    not arrows
    leading to the labia the clitoris
three, carolee schneeman to demonstrate
    orgasm
four, vocabulary lesson:
    c-u-n-t
    v-u-l-v-a

tongue parts
my lips speaks
to all there is
down here

i see i can open
more than ever
first the milk
then my wet arc

this is forbidden language

write the womb
with your fist
curled
a soft finger
try using your lips

i withhold my eggs
all the months of breastfeeding
make pronouncements
by milk and cyprin
by red eczema blooms
on her hands

after the weaning i flare
inside her so she believes
she cannot contain me
then i draw her back
to the rhythm i keep with the moon

they'll call you
essentialist
while the male
philosopher brags
I'm a Lacanian

today we who have birthed
twice with no drugs
curl on the bed waiting
for the meds to kill
the ache of
one failed egg at my centre

can she bear it
the pain it takes
to deliver herself?

to turn to our bodies
looking for our power
it's just not right the professor
hisses we're not talking
about real body parts

don't cast
imagination outside
to make yourself
a non-body
whole and unlacking

that's a man's mistake

in the fort-da *game*
of culture be
persistent
refuse to be thrown
or reeled in

splash of blood
in the bowl
all that red
language
flushed away
before she has
a chance to read it

what's essential:
one, you're in a corner
two, write your own theory
three, use the tools at your disposal:
  an apple a pudding a brush a pen
four, find your centre and push off

giving birth
she touched her power
felt it buzz
like a raw nerve
she knows she is fierce
not only for her children:

i am a woman giving birth to myself

FOUR

happiness threads

We are affirmed by happiness: we go along and get along by doing what we do, and doing it well. Happiness means here living a certain kind of life, one that reaches certain points, and which, in reaching these points, creates happiness for others.—Sara Ahmed

Glossary of abbreviations

BF—breastfeed/breastfeeding/breastfed

BPA—Bisphenol A, an estrogenic chemical in some plastics

BW—babywearing

CD—cloth diapers/cloth diapering

CIO—cry it out

DD—dear daughter

DH—dear husband

DP—dear partner

DS—dear son

DW—dear wife

EUC—excellent used condition

FSOT—for sale or trade

IRL—in real life

LO—little one

MIL—mother-in-law

MILF—mother i'd like to fuck

MT—mei tai (type of baby carrier)

NAK—nursing at keyboard

NIP—nursing in public

OHT—one-handed typing

PM—private message

PPD—postpartum depression; also artist Mary Kelly's *Post-Partum Document*

RS—ring sling (type of baby carrier)

SAHM—stay-at-home mother

WAHM—work-at-home mother

WOHM—work-outside-the-home mother

Thread: welcome!

post by dw on Apr 14, 2009 12:15am

forum

hippie downtown suburban married activist
poor single working yuppie
lounges here where mamas steal a moment
teem + split our online voices
the sameness + difference of our typed selves

usernames + avatars may grin + brag
we post on our children
to posture + compare but this playgroup
is not for them we celebrate
+ confess worry + vent
flex our languid identities
make ourselves not the weary mother hanging
laundry but the bright flags waving on the line
the homemade sparkling castle birthday cake
the magic broom lego mash-up rocket ship
the lumps of play dough we take from our children +
shape
ourselves

Re: welcome!

post by dw on May 2, 2009 11:08 pm

IRL

people talk to me by
asking about my ch☺ldr☺n
h☺sb☺nd's job
the ch☺ldr☺n again
scared to ask something st☺pid like
so what d☺ y☺ d☺?

i have n☺ RL
my ch☺ldr☺n are ☺ll
it's what makes m☺ such a
ha☺☺y ☺bje☺t

i m☺ther anyone who n☺☺ds
to kn☺w there are some things
you can alw☺ys c☺unt ☺n

Re: welcome!

post by dw on May 6, 2009 11:57pm

MILF

mamas at the park call each other hot
                                        not me
am i a prude a haughty
feminist shunning fashion with strict
granola maternity?

maybe
yet when DH mouths sexy to my nakedness
i feel myself
the most exquisite of them all

Re: welcome!
post by wow on May 11, 2009 12:02am

WOW

up-down-up-down
O
up-down-up-down

(flip)

her ☺yes shin☺
tw☺ w☺rds in ☺ne!

m☺mmy f☺und
☺ usern☺me!

Thread: family

post by wow on June 7, 2009 8:54pm

DH

ladies i gotta tell you this one
stumped me at first
H easy enough to decipher
but the D   tricky
for weeks i read your posts like riddles
wrote my own punchlines:

dark + handsome took the kids to the park
damn him, he's out of town again
dweeb husband made supper for once
drunk + hairy slept through the whole thing!

my own D flickered knowingly
through darn + deadbeat to dream
all inside jokes the glossary spoiled

now DH makes every post about him
sweeter   my love
domesticated   steady onscreen so i curse
+ forgive him in each sentence

from another happy housewife

Re: family

post by wow on June 10, 2009 6:41am

DD

i am a big sister   DD's T-shirt

i follow her through the neighbourhood
push the empty stroller while she pounds
her frustration in determined steps

sometimes lose sight of her
find her right beside me too close
to see past DS asleep in the sling

uppy? she whines
an impossible stubborn request
crouch down to hug her
pat her head
offer a snack or some water
we walk some more

Re: family

post by wow on July 5, 2009 10:01pm

DS

bundled baby with the soft head
draws me down with the milk
his weight sways in the sling when i stoop
to lift DD to the swing
to knead the bread

hands busy caring and cleaning i offer
my body as cradle cloth arms to wrap him
offer the thrum of my heart
a breast a breast

postpartum love
divided + rising

Re: family
post by wow on July 13, 2009 1:11am

hint: to find DW see the obituaries

never a DW or a DP
always a straight D
family with a silent W

Re: family

post by wow on Sept 11, 2009 12:17am

dear me

my *i* narrates childbirth recipes MIL horror
worries sleeplessness eczema advice play dates

she gains levels in a maternal
video game while the house digests

i read magazines write no poems
only long posts late at night

Thread: babywearing

post by wow on June 4, 2009 2:16pm

BW

i. wrap*

flash f☺r the camer☺
mama's j☺zz hands they
    ☺ clean
    ☺ cook
    ☺ sew
    ☺ knit

l☺k! sh☺ can ev☺n
s☺☺the a c☺licky inf☺nt while c☺king a glut☺n-fr☺
dinn☺r

**wraps come in a variety of fabrics + lengths use stretchy for an infant woven for older children a simple piece of cloth (SPOC) is an affordable homemade wrap always use a back carry when cooking*

ii. sling**

she can't h☺lp it
s☺ m☺ny styles + f☺brics
winter-weight
s☺larveil for summer
☺nline mama discl☺ses c☺nt☺nts of her thous☺nd-
d☺llar stash

***ring sling padded sling pouch sling used in hip back buddha cradle carrries one over each shoulder for twins—one in the car one in the stroller one in the diaper bag you can never have enough*

iii. mei tai***

b☺hemi☺n mama +
babe turn he☺ds
c☺rrier fet☺sh she
wears like j☺wellery
☺ne for ev☺ry ☺utfit
(hers ☺r b☺by's)

***(*or amautik or chunei or podaegi or rebozo) women around the world wear babies out of necessity we mimic their creativity wear ours to starbucks in solidarity*

Re: babywearing
post by wow on July 21, 2009 8:01pm

RS

july nights i weave through wolseley canvas
empty streets for a breeze
air conditioners whir + drip sweat
sticks a damp cheek to my breast

DS in RS i lunge + hum
past the night baker kneading
snap of caps in the schoolyard
raccoons looking down from the elms
past + past our quiet house
him to sleep

Re: babywearing
post by wow on Sept 15, 2010 7:13am

MT

DS found it the first time
i wore him in an MT
summer day moving
a friend from wolseley to wolseley
him on my back DD in the stroller
basket below her jammed with a toaster
coffeemaker books
i felt him pinch me found blood
later when i put him down

he started day care this fall
each morning said i don't feel so well
i supermanned him up in the MT (one little
hand on moley teddy squished between
his body + mine) to drop
first DD at school then him
supermommed down + so very brave

FSOT Kozy MT in EUC a few
dark stains on one side asking what i paid
$60 PM me if interested

Thread: natural parenting

post by wow on Aug 10, 2009 11:29pm

BF

farts rabbit
carrots like smells + invisible is what
what is invisibile + smells like milk?
DS farts

BF babies + mamas both smell of it
+ look it—child
of slender limbs + milk blistered
lips food stains on his sleeper
from nursing at the dinner table master
of the liquid lunch—mother all breasts
bloated with purpose   body
ragged digesting itself to lay out
mama's all-you-can-eat buffet

too quick with worries
over BPA in the sippy cup
soy in the breastmilk lead paint flaking
in the kitchen
pinned down by a drowsy body a suckling infant
book i read to DD while DS sleeps
my mind flails and panics
CIO to sleep

Re: natural parenting
post by wow on Oct 27, 2009 10:12pm

NIP

we nip in restaurants swimming
pools on the bus we nip wherever we like
nip because we feel like nip
in queues and living rooms
we're cool with nip but nip's still
political for every tender remembering
gaze there's a disgusted one that turns
away there's my MIL at the mall
pretending not to know me

Re: natural parenting
post by wow on Oct 29, 2009 11:22pm

CD

try this: reach into a bucket of shit-piss-vinegar
soaked diapers lift dripping
handfuls into the washing machine
this is why i don't have a front-end loader

my CD smell i refuse to rinse them
the way mom used to
soak shitty diapers in the bowl
plunge her hands in to shake + wring

the mamas say sun bleach them on the clothesline
+ i try
mary kelly of wolseley my mother
psyche on display for the neighbours
a poop-stained painterly PPD

Re: natural parenting
post by wow on Dec 14, 2009 1:24pm

watch

pace me round the 'hood
library play date day care school
clock turns on the swings races
bread in the oven

beat in my ear while the baby nurses
chase boredom through the playground
parse the hours a fevered night
minutes of love and rage
seconds my children growing

watch me
hold on to my wrist
don't let go

Re: natural parenting
post by wow on Dec 2, 2011 10:38am

co-sleeping

chart on my LO's wall marks
12 nights of sleep without me
promises nothing more than 3
rows of stickers yet holds him to his bed like
i never could
mocks 7 years of my broken sleep i wake
in the night missing him spend my days calculating
all a mother can do on 6
solid hours of sleep

Re: natural parenting
post by wow on Mar 5, 2012 7:50pm

instinct

DH exacts my revenge on the mice in the garage
who for weeks it seems have crept
in our car for crumbs
bits of cheese + cookies
left urine + droppings along
the seat behind the boosters
he shows me their corpses
i gasp + gag sleep
better like a good mother wonder
what fabric have i shredded whose food
stolen to feed our pink
mouselets to line a nest for
our tender happiness?

Thread: work-life

post by wow on Feb 20, 2010 8:19pm

SAHM

old women at the thrift shop give free
toys to the children ask
you'll never leave them like those other women
will you?

we are all the sahm family values home-
baked cookies the good
old days written on our bodies

it's nice to think we have nothing
better to do—baby brains—for how else
could we bear the drudgery folding
+ cooking carrying + washing
cycles of motherhood we undo + repeat?

unsatisfied   i am an SAH sham cheerful
like the rest i yell + slam
squeeze too hard feed them smiley
fries + jello go out with puke streaked
in my hair grease stains on my shirt
nag + gripe + blame DH let the kids watch Dora
while i talk on the phone

DH pleads *tell me what you want*
but i have no answer
begin each morning with a vow
to SAH better for my D family

Re: work-life

post by wow on Nov 17, 2010 1:40am

WAHM

every night till two a.m. OHT + NAK
for hours to meet deadlines + soothe
the toddler who must sense it when i bring
my cup of tea to the computer
read the day's posts
sigh
begin

they call this telecommuting
but there's no part of me that
escapes the child's cry smell
of sour milk on my clothes

lucky SAHM with a career i trade my sleep for
organic food in the fridge days at playgroup
gossip at the park PPD that bleeds like
ink from one year to the next i manage until
wahm!
i just can't

Re: work-life

post by wow on Aug 17, 2011 8:03pm

make a list: what do you need in a day care?

1.
remember when you were the perfect
SAHM at the playground
how you gloated over the rough-mannered day-care
kids
the harried workers

2.
why wasn't it enough you ask
when your options are circled
+ crossed out
+ the margins full with calculations
what you can afford

3.
bad. recall how bad when your LO
wakes from a nightmare sweaty begging
you not to go
again when the mamas conclude he's just not
old enough
(too bad for you)

4.
you won't fall for that again
mutilate your desires so he feels no pain
you know what comes naturally can crush you
so even if it hurts
he's going to day care

Re: work-life

post by wow on Jan 10, 2012 7:51pm

WOHM

if you SAH or even WAH go ahead + post it
but never introduce yourself as a WOHM let them
get to know you first see what a great M you are how you can
craft bake volunteer at school like
the rest of them you can throw a mean birthday party

they'll know of course they smell your
guilt + last night's takeout
some will judge you
for processed lunches hours logged at day
care just ignore it your
looking bad is what makes them good

Re: work-life

post by wow on Feb 3, 2012 11:25pm

stretch

time a jog so i won't see
DD on the way from school DS watching
out the window as i pass the day care

halfway to omand's creek i hear it
think of turning back

stay-at-home-alone mom i have stood
in the mouths of their hushed rooms
at our dining-room window watching garbage
recycling trucks workers plant a new tree
but can i watch a train cross the red bridge without him?

no ipod no stroller i plod
a guilty track along the river crest
the hill chug across the bridge alone

whistles sound still far away

Re: work-life
post by wow on Mar 6, 2012 8:34pm

birthday happy

worked late wait forty minutes for a table my hearing
tuned to the fuck-shit of the teenaged greeters'
oblivion to my motherly glare we play
i spy with the brown-on-brown moose
canoe snowshoe woodtones of country hospitality
a simpler life for the urbanite
city treat before the waterslide for the rural kids beside us
slick DD spies green winks of technology in the rafters

in the booth the kids draw people moose
tic-tac-toe on the brown papered table
we order supper at bedtime the server
(who can write her name upside down
but will forget DS's birthday)
mocks me for using the word pilaf
straight from the menu

make a game of chewing brown-edged
lettuce: let's pretend we're robots this is
yummy electricity + oil (mutter to DH
why do the chains have to be so kid
-friendly with the coupons the menus plastic lids
so the chocolate milk won't spill crayons
paper antlers to wear like crowns)

mini ice cream
cones gummy worms forgotten
song we leave their grease
-stained artworks on the
table bundle them out to the car
eyes shining + sleepy sing
every birthday song we know on the way home

FIVE

love poems

I choose to love   this time   for once / with all my intelligence—Adrienne Rich

to a poet

i saw my life swirling in your toilet
pulled it out with bare hands

i cup it here waterlogged
dripping
dear adrienne, what next?

stride

i.

august's dry plenty of time to ponder
the dyslexic adage chalked on a pole near the creek:
there anit no rest for the wicked

is it the homeless pair who doze through rush hour
on a dumpster mattress under the maryland bridge
the summer sun that presses my shoulder
as i tread my rest with the pious
joggers in lulu lemon new balance who wink
from behind designer sunglasses
trot beside their dogs on leashes

anit funny how today
when a road closed sign blocked the way i glanced at
the pole
and thought:
skirt the barricade wicked one
run

ii.

as the geese flew out she
held in long fingers a white farewell

grocery bag flapped and hawksley
crooned autumn's here it's ok now

the elm clings like the fall
we november for once without snow

plastic snaps now cold and tangled only
airplanes head south yet she waves

come snowtime she will fall silent
her beacon broken white on white

iii.

don't touch me i growl
end of a day of cluster feeding
your need does not move me

i set out before the children are sleeping
slide down the river's frozen bank
where the city turns its back

alone i can feel myself all the way to the edges
one human distinct and fully grown

it's love to veer back toward home
tips of my fingers tingling
with all my intelligence

business

i.

sunrise a quick
kiss at the airport
i drive into the dropped jaw of morning

ii.

first day after you left i
wake at 6:40 between both
of the children

sit up to see the clock then
tell them go back to sleep
her arm hurts so i turn us
all over like three wieners rolling on a grill

after that i can't sleep
lie there chuckling: weenies?

come home to us
i'm cracking up

iii.

you are still gone tonight
the house finally
quiet at 9:30 i steal
out to the back yard water
the parched flowers observe
before pulling them down how
the clothes on the line arc with
the garden chimes

the house inhales evening
air and soon the small dreams
sighs upstairs will settle
i climb to the heat of the second floor
shed the day's sweat sunscreen food
-stained clothes and step in the tub

no one wakes yet
for five chill minutes
i lay alone in the leftover bathwater

ancestor

the leaves pressed between
pages of her old bible are fading
their pale skeletons faint
against the aging paper

i only imagine i remember
the silver braids wrapped around her head
and this habit that connects us—
the memories of trees held
in the books we have walked
the folds of our favourite poems
leaving as our prints
thin veins of leaves too ancient to touch
empty spaces our children
fill with stories
our disappearing flesh

petit point (by royal albert)

after the long drive to
edmonton dart to her
bowl lift stones from
water watch the colours
dry

two cups of teeth on the
bathroom shelf salt-and-
pepper collection in the
dining room the house all
doubles: his and hers

my brothers got to eat
sugar cereal grandma had
a whole cupboard full i didn't
care for it chewed all bran
solemnly with grandpa

cigarette saucy in her
wrinkled mouth lipsticked
by a hand i couldn't steady to
paint her nails she liked it
thick coat after coat same
coral as her lips same
arthritic dips and quivers

when grandma looked
she saw stitches in quaint
pinks and blues not the
dizzying pixels i fight
when i look for her
all blurry and overblown

holiday

i.

this morning the knock
knock jokes you yuk-yuks
rattle the house while snow

falls
melts

midair

ii.

bright-red-kool-aid-
dyed-play-dough-caked
knees and beans simmer
all afternoon in your pyjamas
i queen in bed reading to your humdedums

iii.

bedtime i'm tuned to your stories for once all
the way through   laugh
like i've never even heard this one before

iv.

your lullabies and page turns are white
noise
        i sink
into a book notice later the music
stopped   you asleep together
map in one hand
a flashlight beam on a slack
cheek a moving eyelid

X   X

Acknowledgements

To Dad: Mom got the dedication, but you, too, have my love and gratitude.

To Clarise Foster, for the kind of editing some writers only dream of.

Thanks to all the poets who have workshopped my poems, most recently Jennifer Still, Joanne Epp, Angeline Schellenberg, Michelle Elrick, Meíra Cook, and David Streit.

To my friends and collaborators at the Artist Mothers group at Mentoring Artists for Women's Art (MAWA), especially Brenna George, Sandra Brown, Rose Montgomery-Whicher, Devon Kerslake, and Carolina Araneda.

To the mothers of the Winnipeg Babywearers forum, circa 2007, in solidarity.

To my co-workers at *Geez* magazine, for moral support and advice—especially Aiden Enns for helping with the "happiness threads."

And to Heather Milne, Fiona Green, Debbie Schnitzer, Mavis Reimer, Catherine Hunter, Claudine Majzels, and other friends and mentors from the University of Winnipeg.

To Courtney and Sheldon, I wouldn't trade you for anything. And to Jason, my love, thanks for, well, everything.

"my children are not my poetry" was first displayed on the WAM wall at MAWA. "make a list: what do you need in a daycare?" was published in *invisible ink a m/other zine.* "instinct" was published in *Geez* magazine. "ancestor" was published in *Exposed*, edited by Catherine Hunter (The Muses' Company, 2002). "petit point" (by royal albert) was in a show at ArtsJunktion in Winnipeg. Earlier versions of the "happiness threads" were self-published on a special online forum.

Little bird, little pumpkin, and little guy are characters in Vera B. Williams' *More More More Said the Baby* (Greenwillow, 1996), a picture book much loved by my little guy.

Epigraphs come from Debbie Keahey's *Waking Blood* (Turnstone, 2000), Sara Ahmed's *The Promise of Happiness* (Duke University Press, 2010), and Adrienne Rich's *The Dream of a Common Language* (Norton, 1978).